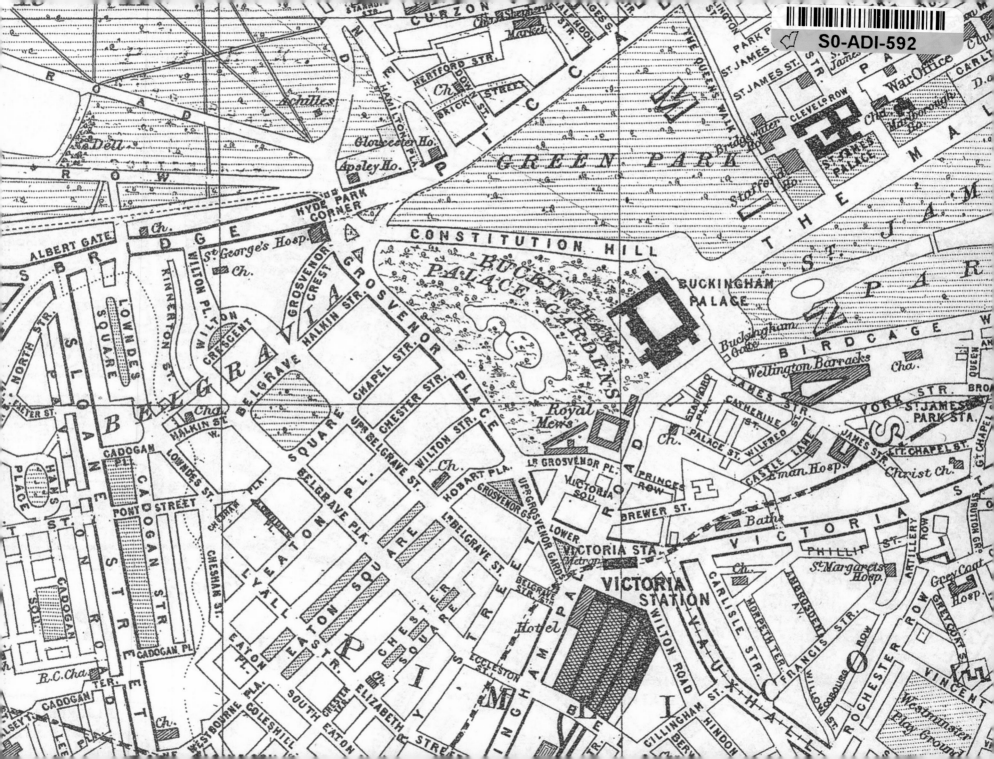

Coventry Kessler
March, 2001

LONDON

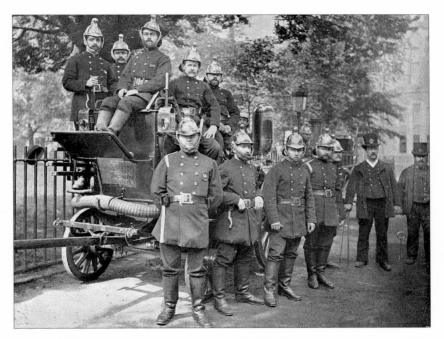

A group of firemen, with engine and turncocks. The Fire Brigade answered 4,111 calls in the year 1894, and saved 122 lives; 845 calls were false alarms.

LONDON

100 YEARS AGO: *a photographic record*

COMPILED BY PHILIPPA LEWIS

PARKGATE
BOOKS

First Published in Great Britain in 1998
by Parkgate Books Ltd, Kiln House, 210 New Kings Road,
London SW6 4NZ

Copyright © Parkgate Books Ltd 1998

Text copyright © Philippa Lewis 1998

British Library Cataloguing in Publication Data:
A CIP catalogue record for this book is available from the British Library.

ISBN 1 85585 368 X (hardback)

Designed by Paul Vater at Sugar Free
Printed and bound in China

The photographs in this book are reproduced from *Around London* published in 1896 by George Newnes of the Strand.

The map reproduced on the end papers is taken from the *'Large Pocket Map of London'*,
first published in 1887 by Charles Baker & Co.

CONTENTS

Introduction

This is a selection from a book of photographs entitled *Around London* published in 1896 by George Newnes of the Strand. The Diamond Jubilee of Queen Victoria was to be celebrated the following year and the publisher probably anticipated good sales from the many people from all over the Empire who flocked to the capital for this year of celebrations and special events. The culmination was on 22 June, when the Queen travelled in a lengthy procession which took her from Buckingham Palace to the City for an open-air service in front of St Paul's Cathedral.

The Times reported that 'the eyes of the whole Empire, and of millions of men beyond its pale will be fixed upon London, and the great and inspiring ceremony with which we celebrate the sixty years of the Queen's reign. They will be fixed upon the revered and beloved figure of the woman who for two full generations has represented to so large a faction of the human race the principles of order, of civilization, of rational progress.'

During those sixty years the face of London had changed immeasurably; not only had all the villages which had previously surrounded London become part of one vast city, but the demands of late nineteenth-century traffic had forced improvements with road-widening and road-building. Streets were lit with gas and electric light and the vestries, which were the local parish councils in London, set up their own electricity generating plants; St Pancras led the way in 1891, followed swiftly by Hampstead and Islington. Other improvements by the Metropolitan Board of Works (which preceded the setting up of the Metropolitan Boroughs in 1899) included the creation of a proper sewage system. The Victorian era had also been one of expanded opportunities for Londoners. These were both social and cerebral, and included innumerable new theatres, schools, institutes, libraries, hospitals, offices, mansion blocks, underground railways, hotels, concert halls and philanthropic organisations.

Walter Besant, who in 1909 wrote a book entitled *London in the Nineteenth Century*, stated the following changes: in 1801 the population was 846,035 but by 1891 it was 4,231,431. 'The century has abolished lotteries, public executions, flogging and imprisonment for debt: it has given baths, public wash-houses, free libraries and free schools, and model lodging-houses to the people; it has extended franchise; it has given the people the right to hold public meetings, to speak as they please, and to form trade unions. It has taken from the people the places where there was formerly every night dancing in public; but it has left the music-halls and the exhibitions. It has opened up for the people a larger and fuller life than they could enjoy before, offering them good music, good pictures, easy access to the country, many holidays and a greatly increased number of theatres.'

Many buildings, both ancient and modern, have not survived the succeeding century; these are marked with a ❖.

Left: A bird's-eye view of London, looking south-east from Bow Church. Cannon Street Station Hotel rises up on the right-hand side of the picture. The spires of the City churches, the Monument and the four turrets of the Tower of London pierce the skyline.

THE RIVER THAMES

At the end of the nineteenth century London was the greatest city in the world, and its position owed much to the river Thames. The Romans built a substantial port in London, since it was the first place that they could establish a viable crossing as they travelled up from the south of England. It flourished as a port from the Middle Ages up to the middle of the twentieth century, and at the time these photographs were taken there was not an ocean of the world where the great sailing ships did not ply their trade.

By the end of the nineteenth century the Thames had ceased to carry much commercial traffic upstream of London. Barges had been replaced by the railway. However, boating for pleasure became hugely popular. Jerome K. Jerome published *Three Men in a Boat* in 1889 and included this description of Moulsey Lock on a summer Sunday: 'I have stood and watched it sometimes, when you could not see any water at all, but only a brilliant tangle of bright blazers, and gay caps, and saucy hats, and many-coloured parasols, and silken rugs, and cloaks, and streaming ribbons, and dainty whites . . .'

Left: *A VIEW OF ST PAUL'S CATHEDRAL from Bankside. It was here that Sir Christopher Wren lived while St Paul's was being built. This would have been his view of the building as he was rowed across the river by the London watermen for the weekly visits that he made during the years from 1675 to 1710, while the cathedral was under construction. The nineteenth-century wharves along the riverbank were principally used by colliers which sailed down from Newcastle bringing coal to the metropolis.*

Left: *The river Thames at the western margin of London: Isleworth, twelve miles from Waterloo Station.*

Right: *A penny steamer plying its trade as it draws up to Lambeth pier, in front of* LAMBETH PALACE, *the official residence of the Archbishop of Canterbury. A day trip on a paddle steamer down the Thames to Gravesend, Southend and Margate was a popular outing.*

The notorious traffic on LONDON BRIDGE which had become so congested by the end of the nineteenth century that a new river crossing from the south bank of the Thames into the City became an absolute necessity: hence the building of Tower Bridge. The traffic was slow and horse-drawn and thousands of people who travelled to work in London from the south had to cross to work in the city from the railway stations on the south bank. Historically, London Bridge had always been popular since it was one of only three bridges that did not charge a toll for crossing, the others being Blackfriars and Westminster. The niches along the bridge became popular spots for 'a curious crowd of idlers composed of small boys, the bona-fide unemployed, and a considerable sprinkling of those who love to behold their fellow-man at work.'

TOWER BRIDGE photographed on its opening day, 30 June 1894. Sir Horace Jones, the architect, and John Wolfe-Barry, the engineer, not only created one of the most celebrated and famous buildings in the world, but solved the problem of pedestrians by building a footway 142 feet above high-water level, reached by means of lifts and stairs within the Gothic towers. The road bridge could be lifted within a minute and half to allow shipping to sail into the Pool of London. This was effected by raising the twin bascules, or drawbridges, each weighing 950 tons, by hydraulic machinery. An observer remarked at the time: 'As might be expected, the panorama from the summit of the main towers is unique, the whole of the mighty, far-reaching Metropolis being unfolded to the beholder.'

Left: *A view over WESTMINSTER BRIDGE to the seven mighty blocks of ST THOMAS'S HOSPITAL ✣ on the south bank. These were opened by Queen Victoria in 1871 after the original medieval buildings were demolished to make way for London Bridge station. It was in this hospital that Florence Nightingale established her school for training nurses. The original Westminster Bridge, finished in 1750, was the second to be built across the Thames, but after problems with the foundations this new one was erected between 1855 and 1862. The consulting architect was Sir Charles Barry, who designed it in keeping with the Houses of Parliament.*

Below: *BLACKFRIARS BRIDGE with the Alexandra Railway Bridge ✣ carrying the London, Chatham and Dover Railway visible just behind. Blackfriars, with its pillars of polished red Aberdeen granite, was considered one of the handsomest bridges in London; it was built in 1864 at the cost of £320,000.*

LONDON DOCKS. The first ship to enter the new London Docks, right, did so in 1805, and for the next twenty-one years all ships coming into the port of London with tobacco, rice, wine and brandy docked there. The warehouses could store 8,316,050 gallons of wine and on a busy day up to three thousand men were employed in the docks to handle the cargoes. All dock work at this time was on a casual basis, with hordes of men seeking work waiting at the dock gates at six o'clock every morning. In 1889, a few years before this photograph was taken, the first dock strike had taken place, with dockers demanding sixpence an hour.

Left: *A view of the dockyard with wine casks. The vaults were described as being 'faintly lit with lamps, and it would appear that parties are every day, and all day long, making exploratory tasting expeditions. For those who taste the wines, the cooper bores the heads of the pipes, which are ranged throughout these vast cellars on either hand in thousands and tens of thousands, and draws a glassful. What cannot be drunk is thrown upon the ground; and it is calculated that at least a hogshead a day is wasted in this manner.'*

Top left: *A view of the* CUSTOM HOUSE *from the river. Its most famous feature was the 190-foot Long Room* (inset) *where customs officials received the documents required by law. (King Ethelred levied the first known customs duty in 979.)*

Right: *A view of the interior of the ivory warehouse at the London Docks and, bottom left, the shell warehouse at Bull Wharf, Queenhithe. 'Nothing will convey to the stranger a better idea of the vast activity and stupendous wealth of London than a visit to these warehouses, filled to overflowing with interminable stores of tea, coffee, sugar, silk, tobacco, and other foreign and colonial products;' so stated the original caption to these pictures.*

London was the principal market for ivory and in 1895 at least sixty thousand tusks were imported from 'Senegambia, Guinea, the Congo, Burmah, Siam, Ceylon, Java and Bombay'. Shells were imported from Australia, India, Tahiti, Japan, New Zealand, Fiji and the Persian Gulf. They were sold to buyers from all over Britain, the Continent and America at sales held six times a year and were used mainly in the manufacture of buttons, but also for mother-of-pearl inlay and knife handles.

THE TOWER OF LONDON

It was William I who first began to build a fortification beside the river Thames, as an expression of power over his newly conquered people. He chose a site on the south-east corner of the Roman city wall. The White Tower (so-called after it was whitewashed during the reign of Henry III) was completed in 1097 and can be seen rising above all the later buildings at the centre of the battlemented walls. Since that time the Tower of London has been a constant backdrop to the march of British history, and the scene of coronations, beheadings, sieges, imprisonments, feasts, tournaments and even royal births. Besides a royal palace it has also been a menagerie for three leopards, a polar bear and an elephant; a mint; the royal armoury; and a place of safekeeping for the royal jewels.

Left: *A bird's-eye view of the whole thirteen acres of the site of the* TOWER OF LONDON, *photographed from the top of Tower Bridge as it was being constructed. This would have been an entirely new sight for Londoners. The poles lying in the river were materials for the construction of the bridge. All building materials used would have arrived by water.*

Inset: *A view of the* TRAITOR'S GATE, *the entrance to the Tower from the river Thames, through which passed many of the Tower's famous prisoners. Anne Boleyn was bought here accused of adultery, imprisoned and then executed exactly three years after her coronation, which had also taken place in the Tower. Queen Elizabeth I, her daughter, famously exclaimed on landing at Traitor's Gate: 'Here landeth as true a subject, being a prisoner, as ever landed at these stairs; and before thee, O God, I speak it.' The ancient gates were removed during a Victorian restoration, and were eventually purchased by the American showman Phineas Barnum from a Whitechapel junk dealer for the sum of £50.*

Left: *Off-duty beefeaters, or, more correctly,* YEOMAN WARDERS OF THE TOWER, *tend their vegetable garden in the old moat. This area was resurrected as a garden during the Second World War as part of the Dig for Victory campaign. Behind them is the Byward Tower, the chief entrance through the outer wall. This, together with the Traitor's Gate and the Beauchamp Tower (to the left of the picture), was built in the second half of the thirteenth century.*

Right: *From the time of the earliest kings the Tower had been used as an arsenal. Records exist, for example, of Henry III asking for twenty-six suits of armour, five iron cuirasses, an iron collar, three pairs of fetters and nine iron helmets to be sent to the Armoury. Henry VIII was particularly interested in armour and made significant additions to the collection. However, by the mid-nineteenth century it was a chaotic jumble of arms dating back five centuries.*

A Victorian expert, Mr Planché, rearranged it for display in chronological order. Shown here is a view of the Horse Armoury. At the centre is the axe which beheaded Queen Elizabeth's favourite, the Earl of Essex, and the block on which Lord Lovat was executed for his part in the Jacobite Rebellion.

THE CITY OF LONDON

This picture was captioned 'the busiest spot in the world': to the left is the Bank of England, in the centre the Royal Exchange and to the right the Mansion House. The commentator continued: 'On a fine summer's day the spectacle witnessed at this spot cannot be matched in any city throughout the world, the whole space in front of these buildings being one slowly-moving mass of vehicles of every description, through which foot passengers make their way as best they can.'

The City is both the most ancient part of London and the traditional centre of the the country's financial matters. On the one hand it has medieval roots in the Guildhall and livery companies - the first mayor was installed in the Guildhall in 1128 - and on the other hand it remains the centre of the City's unique civic government, with its Mayor, Sheriffs and Aldermen who make up its Court of Common Council. The origins of the oldest of the city's livery companies lie in the craft guilds that were formed as early as the twelfth century to protect the standards and prices of their work. The 'livery' refers to the uniforms which evolved for the guild members. The monopolies that they enjoyed brought them great wealth and their concern for the conditions and welfare of their members is the basis of their charitable concerns, which by the end of the nineteenth century was the mainstay of their existence.

Owing to the position of the port on the Thames, merchants had always been based nearby, within the city, together with shopkeepers, small industries and tradesmen. As the century progressed these were replaced by the fast-growing new financial businesses such as banking, insurance and stockbroking. In the middle of the nineteenth century there were 864 brokers, but by 1905 membership of the stock exchange reached 5,567. As the number of offices grew, so the number of residents fell; with increased transport, such as the horse omnibus, it was no longer necessary to live 'above the shop', and increasingly wealthier families moved out of the city to suburbs such as Paddington, Camden Town, Brixton or Clapham.

THE MANSION HOUSE, inhabited since 1753 by the Lord Mayor of London. The Lord Mayor is elected annually and in addition he becomes the Admiral of the Port of London, Chancellor of City University, Head of the Lord Lieutenancy and chairman of the City's two governing bodies. The City was given a charter enabling it to elect its own chief magistrate by King John in 1215, and within the precincts the Mayor has precedence over everyone apart from the sovereign. On ceremonial occasions the Mayor will always meet the ruling monarch at the boundary of the City (previously marked by the City gates) and offer the monarch the hilt of the Pearl Sword, which was a gift to the Mayor and Corporation from Queen Elizabeth I when she opened the first Royal Exchange.

THE BANK OF ENGLAND presents its windowless, secure façade to Threadneedle Street. The bank was founded by a Scotsman, William Paterson, in 1691 and this building was designed by Sir John Soane in 1788. At the time of this photograph it was pointed out that the vaults contained over twenty million pounds in gold and silver, and that at any one time there were over twenty-five million pounds' worth of the Bank's notes in circulation. In the special printing-room about 15,000 bank notes were produced daily. The contemporary description continues: 'The back entrance from Bartholomew Lane is by grand gateway, which opens on to a commodious and spacious courtyard for coaches and waggons that frequently come loaded with gold and silver bullion.'

THE ROYAL MINT moved from the Tower of London in the early nineteenth century to this building on the east side of Tower Hill and was extended in the 1880s to allow for the vastly increased production needed. In one year in the early 1890s the Mint produced 6,898,260 sovereigns, 4,426,625 half-sovereigns, 497,845 crowns, 1,792,600 half-crowns, 1,666,103 florins, 7,039,074 shillings, 7,350,619 sixpences, 3,076,269 threepenny pieces, 8,161,737 pennies, 1,7229,244 halfpennies and 3,904,320 farthings, besides Maundy money and coins for the colonies.

Right: *POULTRY, as the name suggests,
was originally the street where the
poulterers plied their trade. The
surrounding street names, such as
Cheapside, Bread, Milk and Wood
Streets, Honey and Ironmonger
Lanes, attest to the marketing
origins of the whole area. This
photograph shows it still to be a
busy shopping street; however by
end of the nineteenth century
fashionable shopping all took place
in the West End.*

Left: *ST MARTIN-LE-GRAND and the
headquarters of the General Post
Office ✤, a rapidly expanding
institution one hundred years ago,
with its recent Telegraph Department
in addition to letter, book and
newspaper posts and the Central
Savings Bank. 'The number of post
offices and pillars in the Metropolis
is upwards of 2,000 and the number
of people employed in this great
Government institution is about
11,000'.*

Below: *An entrance to the STOCK
EXCHANGE ✤ in THREADNEEDLE STREET,
the brokers and dealers thronging the
pavement. The main entrance to the
building, which was built in 1801 on
the site of an old boxing saloon, was
in Capel Court.*

KING WILLIAM STREET, named for King William IV, whose statue marks the site of the Boar's Head Tavern, which Shakespeare used for the roistering scenes of Falstaff and Prince Henry. Here is the busy junction near Cannon Street railway station and Monument underground railway station.

CITY BOUNDARIES

LUDGATE CIRCUS, *a view up Ludgate Hill toward St Paul's, where the original Lud Gate stood. According to legend the first gate was erected by King Lud in 66 BC. There were subsequent rebuildings, the final one in 1586 incorporating statues of Queen Elizabeth I, King Lud and his two sons. The view up to St Paul's and the church of St Martin, also by Christopher Wren, was famously disfigured by the London, Chatham and Dover Railway Bridge ❖ crossing only 18 feet above the roadway. A contemporary protester described it as: 'an enormous flat-iron lying across the chest of Ludgate Hill like a bar of metal on the breast of a wretch in a torture-chamber.'*

BISHOPSGATE STREET, *the site of one of the original Roman gates to the City of London, rebuilt in succeeding centuries and finally demolished, with all the other City gates, in 1760. At the time of this photograph the site of the gate, at the junction of Camomile and Wormwood Streets, was marked by a large episcopal mitre fixed on the front of the nearest house. The eastern side was called Bishopsgate Street Without.*

THE OLD CITY

CLOTH FAIR *was untouched by the Great Fire of London, the Jacobean houses having their original timber construction intact. Building regulations after the 1666 catastrophe stated that there should be no more overhanging eaves and jetties built of wood. As its name suggests, Cloth Fair's origins lay in the presence of the clothiers and drapers that congregated there from the Middle Ages onwards.*

ST JOHN'S GATE, CLERKENWELL, *a Tudor gateway built in 1504 as an entrance to the ancient Priory of St John of Jerusalem. This was closed down by Henry VIII, who subsequently used the church to store his hunting tents. The rooms above the arch were also turned to secular use: in them Dr Johnson worked on the* **Gentleman's Magazine** *and the famous actor Garrick made his theatrical debut.*

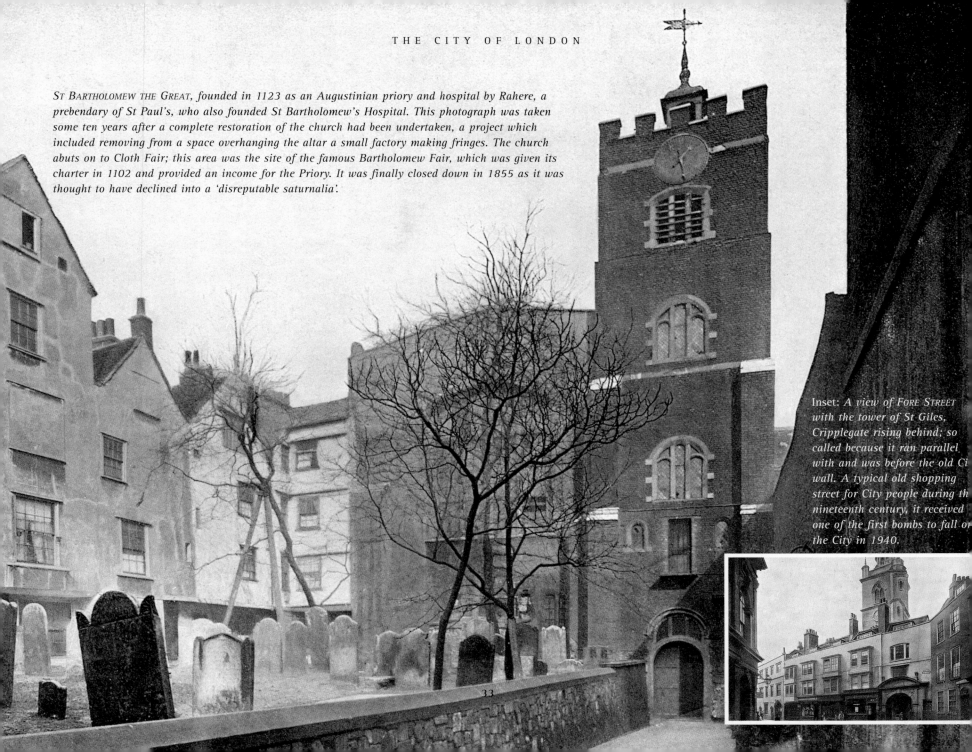

St Bartholomew the Great, founded in 1123 as an Augustinian priory and hospital by Rahere, a prebendary of St Paul's, who also founded St Bartholomew's Hospital. This photograph was taken some ten years after a complete restoration of the church had been undertaken, a project which included removing from a space overhanging the altar a small factory making fringes. The church abuts on to Cloth Fair; this area was the site of the famous Bartholomew Fair, which was given its charter in 1102 and provided an income for the Priory. It was finally closed down in 1855 as it was thought to have declined into a 'disreputable saturnalia'.

Inset: A view of Fore Street with the tower of St Giles, Cripplegate rising behind; so called because it ran parallel with and was before the old Ci wall. A typical old shopping street for City people during th nineteenth century, it received one of the first bombs to fall on the City in 1940.

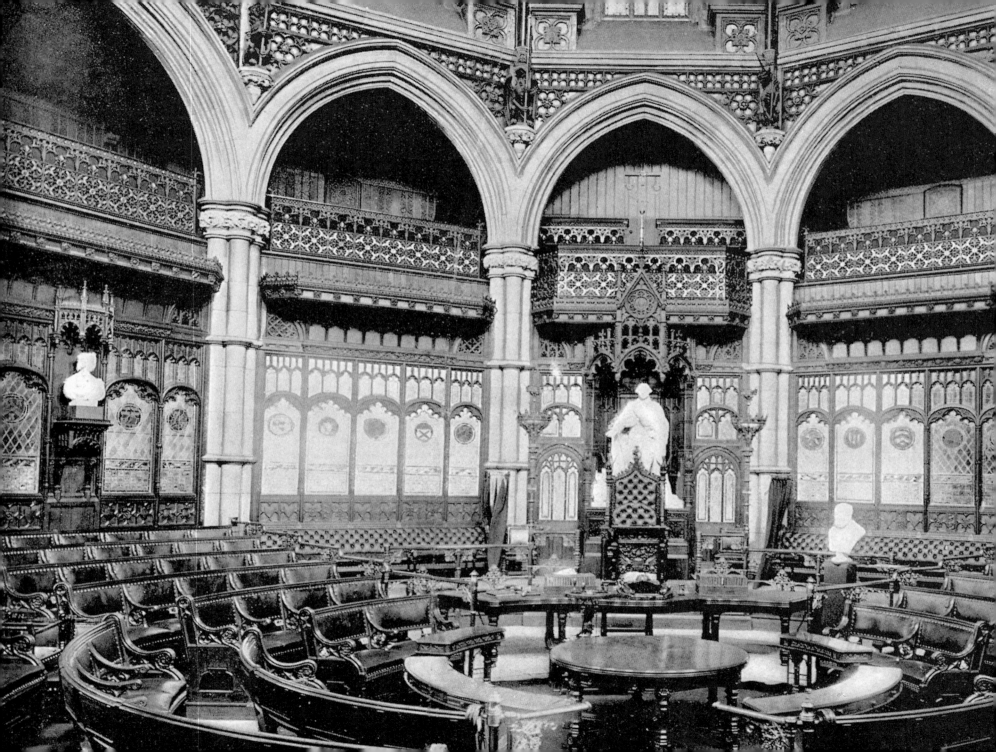

Far left: THE COMMON COUNCIL CHAMBER OF THE GUILDHALL ✤, as it was in the 1890s. Here met the Lord Mayor, twenty aldermen and 236 deputies from the City wards. The centrepiece of the room was the marble statue of George III set in a niche sculptured by Sir Francis Chantrey, who charged the City £3,089 9s. 5d. for it.

Left: The Drawing Room of the MERCERS' HALL ✤ in Ironmonger Lane (which was bombed in 1940). The original mercers were city merchants specialising principally in textiles, exporting wool and importing silks and velvets. This view is of the late seventeenth-century hall which was built after the Great Fire had destroyed the original Tudor hall and chapel. Victorian improvements are in evidence here, instigated by mercers who at that time were patrons of three livings and several schools and hospitals, and gave a number of scholarships to Oxford and Cambridge.

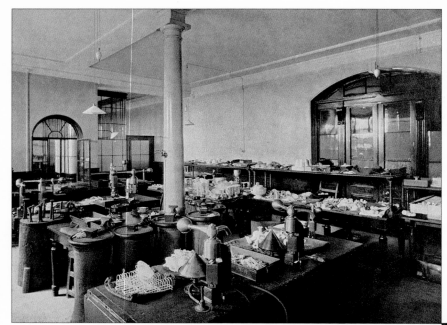

Below: *THE LIVERY HALL OF THE DRAPERS' COMPANY in Throgmorton Street. It was rebuilt in the most grandiose Victorian style, replacing its earlier decor by the Adam brothers. The marble staircase was described as 'fit for a king's palace', the marble pillars, stained-glass windows, carved marble mantelpieces and gilt panelled ceilings as a 'lavish profusion' of 'everything that is rich and tasteful'.*

Above: *The Assay Department of the GOLDSMITHS' HALL in Foster Lane. Unlike many of the Livery companies, the Goldsmiths retained links with the trade that it represented, being described in the original caption to these photographs as 'one of the richest, most ancient and most practical of all the great city livery companies'. It is in the Assay office that items of gold and silver are stamped with a hallmark. This consists of a mark for the place of manufacture (a leopard for London), a letter of the alphabet which indicates the year it was made, the maker's mark, and the Sovereign's head to show that duty has been paid.*

THE DRAWING ROOM and the STAIRCASE OF THE GROCERS' HALL, which was rebuilt in 1893, the fourth hall to be built on the Princes Street site. This was conceived by its architect in the Tudor style, which was probably deemed appropriate since their first hall was opened in 1431; it became famous for its garden, which was open to members of the public. The company was originally called the Pepperers, as pepper was the staple of their trade.

THE EAST END

'PETTICOAT LANE', the market for old clothes and shoes, which ran for two or three miles along Middlesex Street and its neighbouring alleys and back-streets. Henry Mayhew, who wrote about London in the mid-nineteenth century, described it as 'a vista of dinginess. Dress-coats, frock-coats, great-coats, livery and gamekeepers coats, paletots, tunics, trousers, knee-breeches, waistcoats, capes, pilot-coats, plaids, hats, dressing-gowns, shirts, Guernsey frocks, handkerchiefs – all are displayed. The light drab of some aristocratic livery, the dull brown-green of velveteen, the deep blue of a pilot jacket, the variegated figures on the shawls and dressing-gowns, the shine of newly turpentined black satin waistcoats, the glaring green of some flaming tartan – these things, mixed with the hues of women's garments, spotted and striped, certainly present a scene which could not be matched in any other part of the greatest city in the world, nor in any other portion of the world itself.'

While the City of London and the West End were immensely prosperous one hundred years ago, the East End of London became the home to poor, working-class masses; this was partly due to the fact that industries and factories, particularly noxious and stinking ones, were being slowly pushed out from the increasingly grand and financially oriented City. The Docks and all the related trades were also all on the east side of London, with the notoriously rough areas frequented by sailors and dockers. It was to the East End that the waves of immigrants and refugees came in the knowledge that they could find work, however precarious and poorly paid.

Poverty in the East End was of great concern to Victorian philanthropists and church groups who set up 'missions' in the area. One of the foremost was the East London Mission started in 1865 by the founders of the Salvation Army, Catherine and William Booth, with the intention not only of saving people's souls, but also of employing them.

A few years later Blanchard Jerrold in his *London, A Pilgrimage* was describing the East End as 'a spacious township' peopled with 'forlorn men and women, and children from cellars to attics - from the resort of the sewer rat to the nest of the sparrow in the chimney-stack - (who) make up that realm of suffering and crime.'

The broad thoroughfare of the WHITECHAPEL ROAD (far left) was the main route from the City to Essex and therefore was well served with old coaching inns and stables. The infamous slums were in the courts, yards and streets off the main street, and these were made even more notorious by the Whitechapel murders, when six victims were found within a few months during the summer of 1888.

PITFIELD STREET IN HOXTON (left) in the parish of Shoreditch, which was described as an area of squalor and poverty. However: 'residents of more favoured localities would be amazed at the cheapness of the necessaries of life in Pitfield Street. Good meat may be purchased here for 2d. per lb.; and we ourselves have seen apples retailed at 14lb. for 6d.'

A view of SHOREDITCH HIGH STREET (bottom left) on a Saturday morning. The observer notes that one might 'purchase every conceivable article, from fruit and cockles to old books and live birds' from the stalls lining the street. One of the grandest theatres in the East End, the Standard Theatre, was opened on Shoreditch High Street in 1845, offering a combination of variety acts and melodramas.

SOUTH OF THE RIVER

When Queen Victoria ascended the throne the area covered by London was twenty-two square miles. By the end of the century it covered 120. During those sixty years miles of streets were constructed over fields, farms and market gardens. This expansion also occurred south of the river, since the building of new bridges over the Thames had made the area easily accessible. 'There is no open country till one leaves Wimbledon, Streatham, Tooting, even Eltham, well behind', wrote Walter Besant at the beginning of the twentieth century. The advent of the horse-drawn omnibus was a revolution, allowing Londoners to work in the city but live in the new suburbs; by the late 1890s it was calculated that there were 400,000 people commuting to work by train, underground railway and omnibus. Besant analyses the social structure of the new suburbs: Brixton was popular with city clerks, Kennington, Stockwell and Camberwell with city tradesmen, while Balham, Sydenham and Barnes contained 'the richer sort'. The areas closest to the centre were the poorest, and the area around the Borough was considered to be a slum of the worst kind.

While the men went to work in the city, the needs of the families were met locally with the growth of local high street shops, churches and clubs. The first department store in the country, Bon Marché, opened in Brixton in 1877.

Right, inset: *THE HOP EXCHANGE, built in 1865, was the headquarters of the hop trade. This view shows the hall, with its internal ironwork balconies elegantly decorated with hop bines. This is where the business of buying and selling hops took place. Behind were warehouses for storing hops, and adjacent was the massive brewery of Barclay, Perkins and Co., which covered fifteen acres of land and had sufficient stabling for more than two hundred dray-horses.*

Left: *THE NEW CUT, just off Westminster Bridge Road. This was a bustling Saturday and Sunday market in Victorian London, when the cheap shops were augmented by lines of barrows and stalls 'whereon are displayed fruit and greengroceries, villainous-looking sweets, old clothes and furniture, meat at prices ranging from three halfpence a pound upwards, and a strange assortment of articles, such as old locks and keys, door handles, rat-traps, cat's-meat and flowers. When darkness falls the street stalls are lighted by flaring, evil-smelling naphtha lamps.'*

Right: *BOROUGH HIGH STREET, Southwark, on the southern bank, at the approach to London Bridge and on the main route into London from Kent and Surrey. This was one of the busiest spots in London, with traffic both crossing north and travelling to the Borough Market, one of the largest fruit and vegetable markets in the capital and the centre of the hop trade.*

WESTMINSTER

THE TOWERS OF WESTMINSTER: Left to right: BIG BEN, ST MARGARET'S WESTMINSTER, THE WEST FRONT OF WESTMINSTER ABBEY, AND VICTORIA TOWER; a vista encompassing the Abbey and the Palace of Westminster, unified by their Gothic style, if not by their date.

In the foreground is the Westminster Column, a red granite monument erected in the middle of the nineteenth century to the memory of the scholars of Westminster School who died in the Crimea and the Indian Mutiny.

When Edward the Confessor became king, the Pope released him from his vow to make a pilgrimage to Rome on condition that he build a new monastery to St Peter; this he did with the building of Westminster Abbey. He also decided to move his palace to enable him to live next to his new church. William the Conqueror was crowned at Westminster on Christmas Day 1066, and from this period onwards Westminster became the centre of royal power and, subsequently, government.

It was significant that for the coronation of Queen Victoria in 1838 the idea of a splendid cavalcade leading to the Abbey was revived (it had not been performed since the coronation of Charles II), but as a commentator noted: 'the modern one did not traverse the City of London, but that of Westminster, which had now grown larger and more magnificent than its ancient neighbour.' By the time the Queen returned to the Abbey for her Golden Jubilee in 1887, Westminster was even more magnificent, with the addition of the new Houses of Parliament, and the 'official ceremonies were of a magnitude hitherto unapproached in the annals of the nation'.

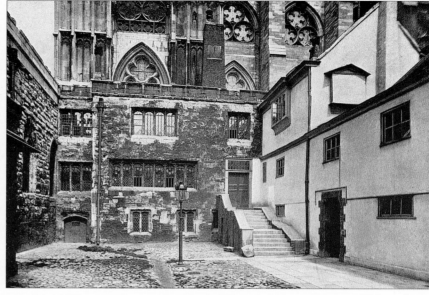

WESTMINSTER ABBEY

Above left: *The Coronation Chairs together with the Shield and Sword of State, both of which were carried in France by Edward III, on display in the 1890s. The Stone of Scone is visible under the oldest of the two Coronation Chairs, which was brought from Scotland in 1297 by King Edward I. All reigning monarchs have been crowned in the chair since this date; even Oliver Cromwell was installed in it as Lord Protector in Westminster Hall on the one occasion that it was carried out of the Abbey. The second chair was made for Queen Mary in 1689, when she was crowned jointly with King William.*

Above right: *An ancient corner of Westminster Abbey, the entrance to the Jerusalem Chamber in the little court of the Deanery. This was originally a guest-chamber for the Abbot's house and was built between 1376 and 1386, but has long been used as the Chapter House. The original abbey chapter house was used by the House of Commons for almost three centuries during the Middle Ages.*

Right: *The interior of the Jerusalem Chamber: the spot where Henry IV died, having been taken ill while praying at the tomb of Edward the Confessor in the Abbey. This view shows it after the 'thorough restoration' of the 1870s during which a fresco of the coronation of Queen Victoria was added to the Jacobean panelling and old tapestries which originally pictured the history of Jerusalem - hence the room's name.*

HOUSES OF PARLIAMENT

A view from Parliament Square.
When the old Palace of Westminster
burnt down in 1834, leaving only
the remains of William Rufus's
Westminster Hall, the great
opportunity for a new building was
seized with enthusiasm. Ninety-seven
different designs in the designated
Gothic or Elizabethan style were
submitted, and it was Charles Barry
who won the competition. 'Big Ben'
was the name given to the principal
bell on the clock (which cracked in
1858 after only two years' use and
had to be replaced). The proportions
are astonishingly grand, the diameter
of the face being 22 feet and the
tower 318 feet high.

THE INTERIOR OF THE HOUSES OF PARLIAMENT *was designed by Barry in conjunction with Augustus Welby Pugin, who ensured that the Gothic style was carried out down to the last door lock and inkwell.*

Top right: *View of the HOUSE OF COMMONS' DINING ROOM 'Thus a member of Parliament who does not take politics too seriously can luxuriate at his ease in the Palace of Westminster . . . and adjourn to the cosy dining-room depicted in this view, feeling sure of the first-class cuisine and service.'*

Bottom right: *The 'splendidly equipped LIBRARY' was another of the rooms provided for the convenience of the members, which were described as having 'all the advantages of a first-class club . . .with every possible convenience.'*

Below: *The HOUSE OF LORDS, which in 1897 had 550 members sitting on its red leather benches. 'The chamber presents a coup d'oeil of the utmost magnificence, no expense having been spared to make it one of the richest in the world.' Queen Victoria's throne is covered by a richly gilded canopy and the smaller chairs were intended for the Prince of Wales and the Sovereign's consort. Since Prince Albert died in 1861 this chair had had little use at the time of this photograph.*

The staircase of the FOREIGN OFFICE, the grandest of all the government buildings, which was finished in 1873. The architect was Sir George Gilbert Scott, who had wanted to design it in the Gothic style, but was forced by the Prime Minister, Lord Palmerston, to use classical Italianate instead. The staircase is decorated in the Victorian manner with potted plants and flowers for a formal reception held by the Prime Minister of the time, Lord Salisbury. Crowds would gather outside the building when there were important functions or Cabinet meetings: 'journalists waiting to get a little descriptive copy, and sightseers desirous of beholding men whose names are on every tongue'.

Right: WHITEHALL, the view north with the Nelson Column rising above all other visible buildings. The massive Treasury buildings on the left of the picture were completed in 1845 to designs by Charles Barry and reflect the growth of government bureaucracy during the reign of Queen Victoria.

53

ROYAL RESIDENCES

A view of BUCKINGHAM PALACE from St James's Park. Queen Victoria moved into the Palace, from the rooms in Kensington Palace that she had shared with her mother, just three weeks after her accession to the throne in 1837, at which point it was reputed to be in an unfinished and rather ramshackle state with extremely smelly drains. Improvements and enlargements, including a ballroom, were made to the original John Nash building and it was properly finished by 1856. The pleasure grounds of Buckingham Palace amounted to forty acres, with a five-acre lake, and the Royal Stables had space for 147 horses.

George IV decided when he ascended the throne that Carlton House, on which, as Prince Regent, he had lavished an immense amount of time and money, was not sufficiently grand for a reigning monarch. He decided to build a new palace on the site of Buckingham House, which had been one of his parents' houses.

Different royal residences had been favoured by preceding monarchs: William and Mary abandoned the Thames-side Whitehall Palace (which soon after burnt to the ground, leaving only the Banqueting Hall extant) and created Kensington Palace for themselves in the 1690s. This and St James's Palace were the principal London residences for succeeding royalty until George III moved to Buckingham House, which he much preferred.

There was much wrangling between George IV and his government as to how much money could be spent on the new Buckingham Palace, and the final bill came to £700,000, excluding the cost of Marble Arch which was designed to be the grand entrance. It was never lived in by either George IV or his successor, William IV.

Left: *The Grand Staircase of*
BUCKINGHAM PALACE, *centrepiece of*
royal and state occasions. 'On the
occasion of a state concert or ball,
the recesses on either side of the
hand-rails are fitted with zinc
holders, which are intended to carry
palms, ferns and choice exotics.
Drawing Room Day sees the whole
extent of the Grand Staircase
simply crowded with ladies in
magnificent dresses, and radiant
with jewels, the whole constituting
a spectacle not easily forgotten.
When we have proceeded up the
first broad flight we find ourselves
on a spacious landing, wherefrom
lesser staircases branch off in
opposite directions. There is also a
flight facing us, and on ascending
by this we find ourselves in the East
or Promenade Gallery. And a
splendid place for promenade is
this, being about 105 feet in length,
brilliantly lighted by electricity, and
provided with luxurious settees and
chairs.'

ST JAMES'S PALACE *was built on the site of an old leper hospital by Henry VIII, who exchanged it with Eton College for another parcel of land. He saw it as a perfect place to build a new mansion and park at the time of his marriage to Anne Boleyn. Much of the Tudor palace was burnt in 1809 save for the Chapel Royal, the gatehouse entrance and the Presence Chamber. Charles I spent his last night here before his execution in nearby Whitehall, and Queen Victoria's accession and marriage both took place at St James's Palace.*

MARLBOROUGH HOUSE, the London home of the Prince and Princess of Wales, which had been given to them on their marriage in 1863. Part of it had previously been used to house the National Gallery. In his younger days the Prince often kept what was perceived as dubious company, in contrast to the decorum of Queen Victoria's Court; the Prince and his friends were often referred to as the 'Marlborough House Set'.

Above left: THE PRINCE OF WALES'S STUDY, a rare photograph since the original accompanying caption to

this photograph pointed out that 'It should be noted that the Prince objects to the intrusion of photographers as a body. Therefore we are extremely fortunate in being able to present here a capital view of His Royal Highness's study, or business room; where it may be truly said, the Prince spends many a busy hour, for our future King has perhaps the largest correspondence of any man in the world.'

Above right: THE INDIAN ROOM, where all the gifts and acquisitions made during his 1875 tour of

India were displayed: 'oriental trophies of every sort - monstrous carved tusks, jewelled daggers, inlaid ivory caskets, damascened armour, quaint little tables, curved scimitars with gem-incrusted gold and silver hilts, and terrible-looking tigers' heads.'

Right: THE ENTRANCE-HALL

Opposite page: THE DRAWING ROOM which was described at the time as 'distinctly modern in character'.

CENTRAL LONDON

The West End, Westminster and the City all had their particular characteristics, but so did the broad streets and surrounding areas that linked these centres, such as the Strand and Fleet Street. A greatly increased city resulted in greatly increased traffic, which city fathers of the Victorian period attempted to resolve with some bold new road schemes, such as the Holborn Viaduct, the Thames Embankment, Shaftesbury Avenue, Charing Cross Road and Queen Victoria Street.

The building of the new Law Courts in the Strand, near to the Inns of Court and ancient Inns of Chancery, concentrated all legal matters in that part of town. An ambitious project, it was ten years in the building and had cost little short of a million pounds by the time it was opened in 1882, but it provided eighteen separate courts, judges' rooms, robing rooms for counsel, jury rooms and accommodation for witnesses. Undoubtedly more wrong-doings were brought to book through the efforts of the growing police force, which doubled in size between the 1860s and 1900, and which had its new headquarters at Scotland Yard.

The area around Fleet Street was the centre of the newspaper and publishing industry. Newspaper tax was abolished in 1855, and the gradual decrease in the price of paper stimulated considerable growth in newspapers, journals, books and magazines, which were published in ever increasing numbers.

Above: *In 1891 New Scotland Yard was opened, a tangible sign of the burgeoning police force. This building by Norman Shaw replaced the row of old houses that had been used as offices since Sir Robert Peel had founded the Metropolitan police force in 1829; these had been partially destroyed by a Fenian bomb in 1883. New Scotland Yard was built in granite quarried by Dartmoor prisoners, red brick and white stone, which appeared strikingly different from the stone buildings which surrounded it.*

Below: *THE NEW BANKRUPTCY COURTS* ♣, finished in 1892 and viewed from St Clement's Gardens off the Strand. England was during this period the 'workshop of the world, with an extraordinary multiplicity of manufacturing businesses. Inevitably as commerce expanded greatly so did the number of failures, hence the need for a new larger court for bankrupts. 'On entering the building by one of these portals, the visitor finds himself in a very long broad corridor, which is crowded daily with learned expounders of our bankruptcy laws and their clerks, and is constantly the scene of bustling activity.'

STAPLE INN AND BARNARD'S INN were both Inns of Chancery. These foundations dated from the medieval period when they were educational establishments for students wishing to be called to the Bar; later they became merely clubs for attorneys and solicitors. Originally there were eight such inns, but most were demolished or sold off during the nineteenth century. The view of Staple Inn shows the gateway which led into the two courtyards. The American writer Nathaniel Hawthorne described it: 'There was not a quieter spot in England than this, and it was very strange to have drifted into it so suddenly out of the bustle and rumble of Holborn. . . . . In all the hundreds of years since London was built, it has not been able to sweep its roaring tide over that little island of quiet.'

BARNARD'S INN was the smallest of the Inns of Chancery, with a hall only 22 feet wide. When Charles Dickens wrote Great Expectations *his hero Pip describes the place as 'the dingiest collection of shabby buildings ever squeezed together in a rank corner as a club for Tom-cats . . . 'I thought it had the most dismal trees in it, and the most dismal sparrows, and the most dismal cats, and the most dismal houses that I had ever seen. I thought the windows of the sets of chambers into which those houses were divided, were in every stage of dilapidated blind and curtain, crippled flower-pot, cracked glass, dusty decay, and miserable makeshift'. In 1892 the Mercers' Company bought the building for their school.*

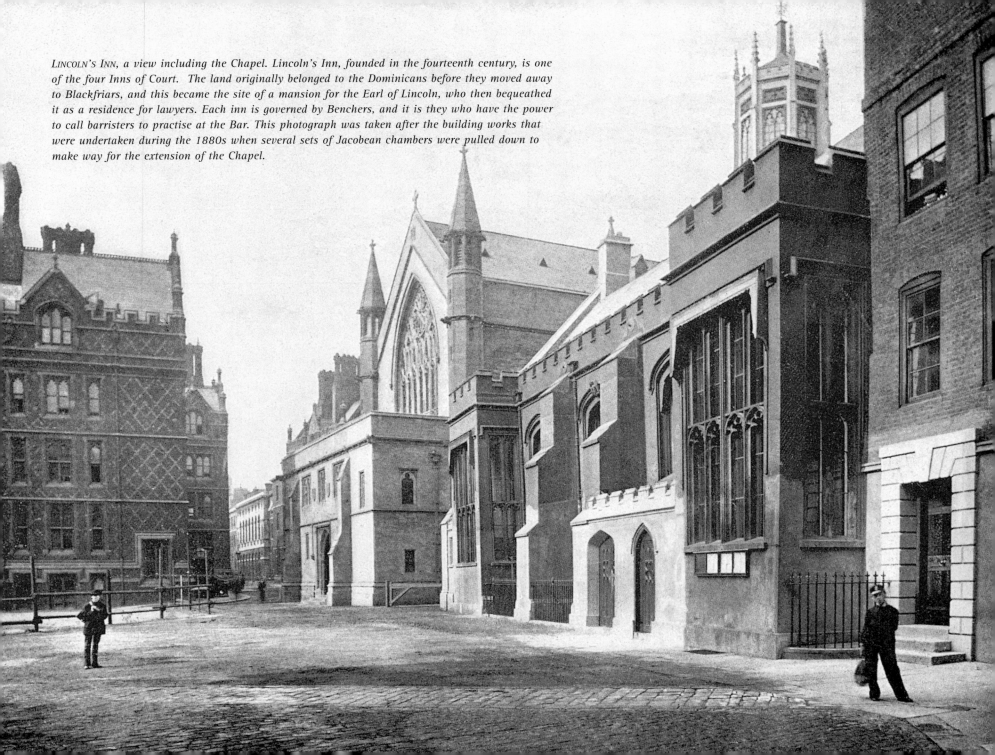

LINCOLN'S INN, *a view including the Chapel. Lincoln's Inn, founded in the fourteenth century, is one of the four Inns of Court. The land originally belonged to the Dominicans before they moved away to Blackfriars, and this became the site of a mansion for the Earl of Lincoln, who then bequeathed it as a residence for lawyers. Each inn is governed by Benchers, and it is they who have the power to call barristers to practise at the Bar. This photograph was taken after the building works that were undertaken during the 1880s when several sets of Jacobean chambers were pulled down to make way for the extension of the Chapel.*

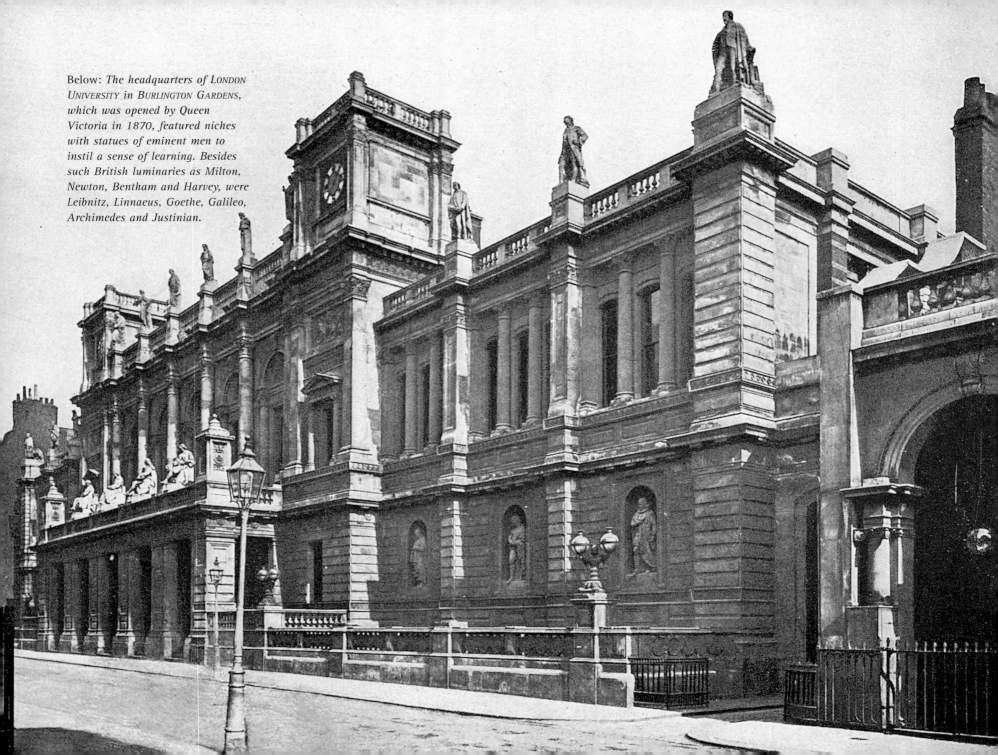

Below: *The headquarters of* LONDON
UNIVERSITY *in* BURLINGTON GARDENS,
*which was opened by Queen
Victoria in 1870, featured niches
with statues of eminent men to
instil a sense of learning. Besides
such British luminaries as Milton,
Newton, Bentham and Harvey, were
Leibnitz, Linnaeus, Goethe, Galileo,
Archimedes and Justinian.*

Right: *City of London school on the Thames Embankment between White and Blackfriars, photographed shortly after the opening of its new building by the Prince and Princess of Wales in 1882. It was described as being 'in the style of the Italian Renaissance with polished columns of Aberdeen granite'. The niches on the exterior were filled with statues of Shakespeare, Milton, Bacon, Newton and Sir Thomas More, none of whom had anything to do with the school since it was founded in 1837 in Milk Street for the 'sons of respectable persons engaged in commercial, professional or trading pursuits.'*

Below: *The pupils of Christ's Hospital ♣ on parade in front of the hall just before the school moved its premises out of the City of London to Sussex in 1902. The institution was founded in 1553 by Edward VI for the care of orphans but developed into a school for both girls and boys. Sir Christopher Wren rebuilt many of the buildings destroyed by the Great Fire of London and the girls were moved to Hertford in 1704. The uniform remained almost unchanged from the Tudor period: a long dark blue surcoat and bright yellow stockings (hence the name Bluecoat boys).*

Left: *SMITHFIELD MEAT MARKET*; there
are records of 'Smoothfield', a
grassy space outside the city walls
where animals were traded as early
as the twelfth century. This
building, a model of Victorian
organisation, had an extensive
railway depot belonging to the Great
Western Railway built underneath
it, complete with lift to take the
meat down to the trucks. There was
a separate building for pork, poultry
and provisions.

Right: *COVENT GARDEN MARKET*,
which took place on Tuesdays,
Thursdays and Saturdays, starting
in the early hours of the morning
when the market men famously
coincided with people dining late
after the theatre or opera.

Opposite: NEW OXFORD STREET, *looking down towards Holborn. The street was created in the 1840s, making a direct route from Oxford Street through to Holborn. It drove through what had been some of the most notorious slums in London, the St Giles 'Rookery'. The street at this point is dominated by the headquarters of Messrs A. and F. Pears* ❖*, soap manufacturers, described at the time as a 'truly palatial establishment'. Pears was one of the best-known brand names of the Victorian period owing to their prodigious advertising. Their most famous image was the painting commissioned from Sir John Everett Millais entitled 'Bubbles'. The building in the process of demolition farther down the street is the Bedford Chapel* ❖*.*

Left: *A view of* HOLBORN, *looking west. The large building in the centre of the picture, and opposite the entrance to Chancery Lane, is the First Avenue Hotel* ❖*. It was one of the many hotels recently erected in the capital, and was described as 'not so pleasantly situated' but 'not nearly so expensive' as many of the others.*

FARRINGDON STREET, *a view showing the Holborn Viaduct. This street runs along the course of the Fleet river, which had become by the eighteenth century not much better than an open sewer and rubbish dump. It was therefore covered over and so Farringdon Street was created. Subsequently, its narrowness caused problems for the traffic crossing Blackfriars Bridge into London and it had to be widened in the early nineteenth century.*

HOLBORN VIADUCT, *a view looking towards Newgate Street. The Viaduct, opened by the Queen in 1869, was one of the major improvements to Victorian London. Previously the traffic had had to descend the narrow Holborn Hill in order to cross what was, in fact, the valley of the river Fleet. The high-level viaduct bridge, which crossed over Farringdon Street, created a spacious new thoroughfare linking the two commercial centres of the City and the Holborn, Oxford Street area. Aptly, the viaduct was ornamented with statues representing Commerce and Agriculture on the south side, Science and Fine Art on the north.*

NORTHUMBERLAND AVENUE *and* WHITEHALL PLACE, *a photograph taken from the Victoria Embankment. With the massive undertaking of creating the Thames embankments came opportunities for grand new building schemes on reclaimed land that had previously been muddy river banks. The National Liberal Club, on the left, was opened in 1887 and its sumptuous interior marble decoration was much admired. It was established to create a centre for Liberal politicians from all over the country. Adjoining it, was Whitehall Court which consisted of that relatively new phenomenon, the flat. The Metropole Hotel, at that point the largest hotel in London with over seven hundred rooms, was built opposite.*

FLEET STREET had been the centre of London's printing and publishing industry since Tudor times, when one of England's earliest printers Wynken de Worde opened for business in about 1500. In the 1890s it was still the centre of the newspaper and publishing industry and the following words described this view: 'within half a mile from this point some of the greatest newspapers in the world work and think for millions of readers . . . good, honest, hard work is done in and about Fleet Street, and goes forth to the whole English-speaking race.' Fleet Street was also famous for its taverns.

Far right: *OFFICE OF THE TIMES* ✤ *in Queen Victoria Street, which at that date had been printed and published on the same site since 1788. It was founded in 1785 by John Walter, whose first name for his paper was* The Daily Universal Register. *In the 1890s the newspaper was printed in Printing House Square which lay behind these offices, and it was calculated that for every edition the compositors put together two and a half million separate pieces of metal type. A record number of 110,000 copies were sold of the paper which covered the marriage of the Prince of Wales.*

THE WEST END

The West End of London, as opposed to the financial centre of the city to the east, was the fashionable area of London. The linchpin of society was the monarch, and since the medieval period the Royal Family had lived to the west, rather than the east, of the city. The penumbra of the Court fell within close proximity of the royal palaces, and fashionable society moved away from the city – first to Bloomsbury, then to Mayfair, and finally, in the nineteenth century, to Belgravia. By the 1890s Knightsbridge and the areas north of Hyde Park were also socially acceptable.

The Season ran from Christmas to July, and when it finished many of the workers in the West End, the domestic servants, the dressmakers, the laundresses and the flower-sellers were summarily dismissed. Many of them lived nearby, north in Marylebone or east around Seven Dials, where the publisher of these photographs noted 'you may moralize on the startling extremes of squalor and splendour that are met with even in the West-end of London.'

The people who comprised 'Society' were described by Blanchard Jerrold in his *London, A Pilgrimage* of 1872 as the minority: 'The non-workers, those who are able to choose, or are compelled to live without labour; but they are powerful by their culture and wealth . . . Princes and princesses of fashion; the observed of all observers at Court and Drawing-Rooms; the peerless beauty and the most engaging of men . . .'

PICCADILLY, looking East from Green Park. Accompanying this picture in 1896 is the caption: 'In the height of the London season, this particular part of Piccadilly is thronged with elegant carriages, while distinguished men, whose names are household words throughout the world, may be seen strolling towards Hyde Park and Piccadilly Circus, or else conversing on the steps of the palatial clubs . . . Most of the streets that lead out of Piccadilly on the left bring one to the heart of Mayfair, a district which may be safely described as the most aristocratic part of the Metropolis.'

CLUBLAND

Above left: *St James's Street, where many of the older London clubs were situated: Boodles and White's on the east side of the street, and Brooks's on the west. These clubs had been the scene of riotous living and gambling during the eighteenth century; the clubs founded in the nineteenth century tended to have more elevated purposes, such as the discussion of politics or travel.*

Above right: *Pall Mall with a view of the Carlton Club, which was built in 1856. Traditionally this was the power base of the Conservative politicians and one of Queen Victoria's favourite prime ministers, Benjamin Disraeli, was a member. As a late nineteenth-century commentator put it: 'The grand mysterious tactics of the General Election are decided upon here, and within these walls are subscribed the vast sums which are to put the whole forces of the Conservative party in motion.' At that date election to the club was vetted by the committee and cost members £30 with an annual subscription of eleven guineas. Beyond the Carlton Club is the Reform Club, headquarters of Liberal politicians.*

Right: *The Constitutional Club ♣ in Northumberland Avenue. The new 'German Renaissance style' wedge-shaped building opened its doors in 1886 and reported ten years later that it had six thousand members and a staff of over two hundred, a fact which probably reflects the vast popularity of gentlemen's clubs and how they fitted into the social scene of the day. The street was built after Northumberland House, the town mansion of the Duke of Northumberland, was demolished and the land sold off in the 1870s.*

WEST END SHOPPING
Above: *THE QUADRANT* ♣, *REGENT STREET;* this was part of the scheme designed by the Prince Regent's architect, John Nash, to link his newly built terraces in Regent's Park to his palace, Carlton House. It had the effect of extending the fashionable area of London eastwards, and housed some of the finest shops in the capital. Two to four o'clock in the afternoon were the fashionable shopping hours: a description of Regent Street during the season in the Illustrated London News recounts that 'the brilliant ever-shifting scene presented daily is dizzying in its confusion. On days of court ceremonial strings of carriages filled with beauty, rank, and fashion, creep at a snail's pace towards St James's or Buckingham Palace. At other times, the fireflies of fashion glance rapidly hither and thither, and the West End streets are thronged with the promiscuous jungle of carriages, horsemen and horsewomen, cabs, omnibuses and wagons; the pavements being crowded with fashionable loungers. With what dignified ease the gorgeously bedizened footmen attend to their mistresses or lounge about in attitudes of studied grace.' Out of season, Regent Street was described as 'gloom and desolation'.

Top: *BOND STREET*, a view looking towards Oxford Street. This had been one of the most fashionable shopping streets since the late eighteenth century. A century later it was still described as consisting mainly of fashionable shops 'which are patronized almost exclusively by the nobility and wealthy classes generally. On a fine day in May or June this street is simply jammed with splendid equipages, while the crush of fashionable folk on the footways is equally dense.' So notorious were the traffic jams in Bond Street that shops who had them, advertised their entrances in side streets, such as Conduit Street.

Bottom: *OXFORD STREET* was one of the longest streets of shops in London, the western end being considered far smarter than the eastern. It never had the social cachet of Regent Street and Bond Street, since it bordered less salubrious parts of town such as Soho. In 1876, in order to keep the noise down, Oxford Street and several other West End streets were entirely paved with wooden blocks set in bitumen. Granite paving was considered 'impossibly noisy'.

Top: *PARK LANE contained some of the grandest town houses in London, including Gloucester House* ✤ *which belonged to the Duke of Cambridge (who, had he been born a few months earlier, would have inherited the throne from the childless William IV, rather than Victoria) and Holdernesse House, residence of the Marquess of Londonderry. Its junction with Piccadilly, hitherto very narrow and impossibly crowded, was improved by the creation of Hamilton Place in the 1870s. The ornamental fountain on the right was then erected at the turning; it incorporated heroic marble statues of Shakespeare, Milton and Chaucer topped by the figure of Fame. The cost of £5,000 was met by money collected by the government from the property of an intestate old lady.*

Right: *HYDE PARK CORNER, a view looking at the arched screen entrance to Hyde Park, with the Duke of Wellington's Apsley House beyond. This entrance was designed by Decimus Burton and erected in 1825, in place of the turnpike gates marking the entrance to London that stood there before. This explains Apsley House's famous address of No. 1 London.*

Right: *PALL MALL viewed from the bottom of St James's Street. The Prince of Wales's Marlborough House opened on to Pall Mall. The fact that so many clubs were in the immediate vicinity meant that it was a very popular address for sets of private residential 'chambers' which were considered suitable and correct lodgings for bachelor gentlemen and men-about-town.*

OXFORD CIRCUS, *the intersection of Oxford and Regent Streets, two of London's most popular shopping streets, and a destination of horse-drawn omnibuses from surrounding areas and suburbs. These were introduced during the 1850s, and remained a feature of London traffic together with the hackney cab. They were displaced in some areas by horse-drawn trams which were faster and cheaper.*

TRAFALGAR SQUARE at the end of the last century when the skyline was dominated by the 145-foot Nelson Column, erected by public subscription in 1843. The statue of Nelson itself is 17 feet high, and the capital of the vast column was made from a bronze cannon captured by him from the French.

PICCADILLY CIRCUS, in the foreground the fountain erected to the memory of Lord Shaftesbury. A public subscription raised money for the monument in recognition of the work achieved by the philanthropist Lord Shaftesbury; this included an act abolishing the employment of boy chimney sweeps, a law ensuring factory workers only worked a ten-hour day, the abolition of children and women working in the coal mines and 'ragged' schools for the poor. He died in 1883, and the statue was unveiled ten years later. It was intended that the figure should represent the angel of Christian Charity, not Eros, the god of Love. In the background is the London Pavilion, at that period a new theatre famed for its variety programmes.

PLACES OF ENTERTAINMENT AND SPECTACLE

Left: *The Empire Theatre* ♣,
Leicester Square, the most famous
variety theatre in London and one
where 'the entrance does not convey
an adequate idea of the
magnificence of this theatre, which
may be described as the elysium of
the jeunesse dorée . . . no one can
deny the dazzling brilliance of the
scene which the interior of the
Empire presents at, say, 10.30 p.m.;
no wonder that the Empire lounge
should be the favourite resort of the
Oriental potentate in London.' The
major part of the performance was
a ballet performed by girls in flesh-
coloured tights, which moral
reformers of the 1890s considered
to be the very depths of depravity.
The newly-formed London County
Council demanded, famously, that a
screen should be erected preventing
theatre-goers drinking and
socialising in the promenade area
from seeing what was happening on
the stage. This caused outrage
among the patrons, among them a
young Winston Churchill, who
pulled it to pieces on the first night
that it appeared.

At the end of the nineteenth century, there was no shortage of places for the Victorian to visit. There existed a general desire for improvement and education, and concerts, lectures and sermons at the many public halls became part of life for the middle and upper classes. Museums were flourishing with the newly created Natural History Museum and Victoria & Albert Museum in South Kensington delighting the visitors.

The theatre had become a far more respectable place. Until the second half of the century the pit had been a seething mass of vociferous play-goers interspersed with women selling oranges, nuts, ginger beer and stout from large baskets. These had been replaced with the comfortable and expensive stall seats, whose patrons were described by the journalist G.A. Sala in 1894 as a 'thickly-packed assemblage of gentlemen in faultless evening dress, the majority of them with gardenias or carnations in their button-holes, and the ladies in ravishing toilettes.' Variety theatre and music hall were another popular, albeit not so respectable, option. These took place in opulent buildings which were designed to enable smoking and drinking while the performance was taking place.

Pubs had also changed; since railway travel had ousted the long-distance stage coach, old coaching inns with their large stable yards became redundant; they were replaced by the spacious new Victorian pubs glittering with glass, brass and polished wood.

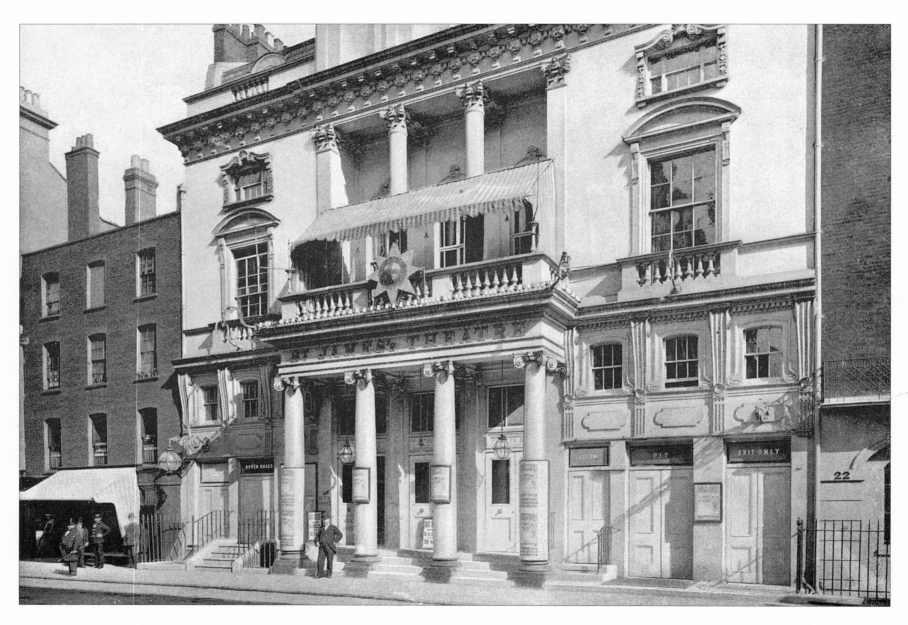

THEATRES

ST JAMES'S THEATRE ♣ was built in 1835. It was not very popular until it came under the management of George Alexander in the 1890s. This was where many of Oscar Wilde's most successful plays were first performed, notably Lady Windermere's Fan *in 1892, where on the first night one of the central characters and many of Wilde's friends in the audience all wore green carnations. In his curtain-call speech on the first night Wilde announced: 'I must tell you I think my piece excellent. And all these puppets that have performed in it have played extremely well. I hope you like my piece as well as I do myself.'*

ALHAMBRA THEATRE ♣, a view from across the gardens of Leicester Square. The Moorish style Alhambra Theatre was rebuilt after a fire in 1883 had destroyed the original building, and set itself up as the rival variety theatre to the Empire. Its main attractions were its scantily clad ballet dancers, described by an enthusiast as 'poetry in motion', and its orchestra second only to that of the Royal Opera House.

HALLS

Above: *QUEEN'S HALL* ✣ *IN LANGHAM PLACE*; built in 1893 'to meet the growing musical demands of the Metropolis' it was designed with two concert halls, one for large orchestral concerts and one for chamber music. However, like most Victorian halls of this type it was also used for balls, wedding receptions, bazaars, lectures and banquets. It was here in 1895 that Henry Wood was appointed conductor of the Queen's Hall and inaugurated a series of promenade concerts, which became an instant success, in the October of that year.

Left: *THE ROYAL ALBERT HALL*, a view from the Albert Memorial, two of the buildings which were the national expression of honour to Queen Victoria's dead consort. In the 1850s Prince Albert had mooted the idea of a large hall for concerts, lectures, libraries and exhibition rooms and a design had duly been produced by a Captain Fowke, of the Royal Engineers, for a hall intended to hold 15,000 people. However the scheme was shelved until after Albert's death in 1861. Fowke's original plans were adapted by Colonel Scott, also of the Royal Engineers, and the Queen finally laid the foundation stone in 1867. The organ was famed for its enormity, having 10,000 pipes.

Above: *THE AGRICULTURAL HALL* in Islington covered an area of at least three acres; it was originally established by members of the Smithfield Club who held their first cattle show in the December of 1862. An annual horse show was held each summer during the week between Epsom and Ascot races, and a military tournament every June. Over the Christmas holidays it was famous for its indoor fair with swings, shooting galleries, roundabouts, circus, side-shows and menagerie. For the last twenty years of the century the vastly popular Mohawk Minstrels were a regular feature in the Grand Concert Hall which was incorporated in the Agricultural Hall.

Right: EXETER HALL ♣ had been built as a meeting place for scientific discussions and religious gatherings in 1830; its worthy purpose was retained when it was acquired by the Young Men's Christian Association during the 1880s. They enlarged the building with the addition of class-rooms and a gym together with 'the nearest approach to an ideal restaurant, the waiters being the very embodiment of meekness and civility.' This was also the venue for the 'May Meetings', a series of sermons, devotional gatherings and improving lectures which were held every spring, and which were considered by some to be a feature of the London season.

Below left: THE METROPOLITAN TABERNACLE ♣, a view of the interior which was generally known as 'Spurgeon's Tabernacle' since it was built for the phenomenally popular Baptist preacher Charles Spurgeon. He first preached in London at the age of 19 in 1853 and was soon filling the Surrey Gardens Music Hall on Sunday nights when it was temporarily converted for religious services. He also regularly preached at Exeter Hall, newspapers announcing that 'the Strand was blocked up by crowds who gathered to hear a young man in Exeter Hall'. His congregation raised £31,000 to build the Tabernacle and there was room for 6,000 people 'without excessive crowding', a lecture hall for 900 and a schoolroom for 1,000 children.

Right: THE NATURAL HISTORY MUSEUM, designed by the architect Alfred Waterhouse, was opened in 1881. This is a view of the south-east gallery for the study of mammals, and dominated by a skeleton of the mastodon from Missouri, U.S.A. Other wonders described at the time included the skull of a megatherium from Buenos Aires, the skull of a dinotherium from Hesse-Darmstadt and 'wonderfully carved bones' from prehistoric cave dwellers.

PLACES OF AMUSEMENT
Left: *THE CRYSTAL PALACE* ♣ *in Sydenham, described during the 1890s as one of the best and cheapest places of amusement in London, when it was not unusual for sixty to eighty thousand people to visit it in one day. Joseph Paxton's glass and iron structure was created for the Great Exhibition of 1851 and moved from Hyde Park two years later. Its many attractions included a magnificent park and grounds, fountains and firework displays, and a viewing platform on the north tower from which one could see across seven counties. The interior included the Great Nave with marble basins and waterlilies, glass fountains, groups of statues, the Grand Orchestra with space for 4,000 performers and the Grand Organ.*

(Right) THE GREAT WHEEL AT EARL'S COURT ♣, *from which 'all London is spread before the passenger in the topmost car, and on a clear day even Windsor Castle is distinctly visible.' In 1896 this wheel was taken to be the largest wheel in the world at over 300 feet high; there were forty cars and each one held thirty to forty people. The wheel was part of an entertainment ground opened by a Mr Whitley in 1887 who also staged spectaculars such as Buffalo Bill's Wild West Show on the site.*

THE PEOPLE'S PALACE ✤ in the Mile End Road was opened by Queen Victoria in the year of her Golden Jubilee, 1887, with the following words: 'It gives me great satisfaction to open this fine building provided for the people of the East End of London, whose lives of unceasing and honourable toil will be cheered by the various opportunities of rational and instructive entertainment and of artistic enjoyment here afforded to them.' The Palace included a great central hall, library, swimming-baths, technical, trade and science schools, gymnasia, billiard and refreshment rooms, great exhibitions, winter gardens and much more.

THE ROYAL AQUARIUM ♣, which appears on the right-hand side of this view, had the unique feature of thirty vast fish tanks, as well as the more usual attractions of sculpture, an orchestra and palm trees in the main hall. However the aquarium was not a successful venture, and Mr Josiah Ritchie turned it into a music hall with a speciality of freakish turns, such as Zulima, the Strongest Woman in the World, who was appearing when this photograph was taken. Genuine Zulus also appeared, and a girl called Zazel was fired from a cannon. The building at the end of Tothill Street, which ran along the side of the Aquarium, was Queen Anne's Mansions, which at fourteen storeys high was at this time the tallest domestic building in London.

Left: THE TABARD INN in SOUTHWARK ♣, *a view of the courtyard just before it was demolished with apparently little regard to the fact that it was the site where Geoffrey Chaucer and his fellow pilgrims met on their journey to Canterbury, and where they feasted before setting off: 'Our host gave us great welcome; everyone / Was given a place and supper was begun./ He served the finest victuals you could think, / The wine was strong and we were glad to drink.' It ceased to be an inn in 1873 and was then used, as can be seen here, as a luggage and shipping office.*

Right: THE GEORGE INN was another of *the historic inns which clustered in Southwark. This was no doubt because in the period prior to 1729 London Bridge was the only place to cross the river if you were travelling up from the south. Dickens particularly admired these old inns and wrote: 'In the Borough, especially, there still remain some half-dozen old inns which have preserved their external features unchanged, and which have escaped alike the rage for public improvement and the encroachment of private speculation. Great, rambling, queer old places they are, with galleries, and passages, and staircases, wide enough and antiquated enough to furnish material for a hundred ghost stories.'*

Left: THE HORSE SHOE TAVERN, TOTTENHAM COURT ROAD, which began as the pub attached to the vast Meux's brewery ♣, the entrance to which is just visible in front of the pub. When this photograph was taken the pub had just been transmogrified into a hotel with a horse-shoe-shaped dining room.

Below: ANGEL, ISLINGTON ♣, the site of a coaching inn since the seventeenth century, and a noted staging post for mail coaches travelling between London and the Great North Road. As it was always such a famous and busy spot, the Angel was frequently rebuilt and modernised. The original inn was demolished in 1819 to make way for something larger, and this in turn was enlarged in 1880, as one commentator noted: 'Instead of low, old-fashioned wainscoted parlours, filled with country guests and northern graziers, we have the usual characteristics of a modern London tavern – glittering plate-glass, and spacious, splendid bars with costly fittings quite in keeping with the importance of the house as one of the great landmarks of London.' The northern graziers he refers to would have been herding their sheep and cattle to the market at Smithfield, making their way down St John Street which led south off this junction.

The Viaduct Tavern, named for the Holborn Viaduct which was built in 1869 to connect Holborn with Newgate Street. Many Victorian pubs were built on important junctions and corner sites in order to make the maximum impression. At night the vast gas lamps illuminated the huge letters and would have made the cut and etched glass windows glitter. Opposite the Viaduct Tavern is Newgate Gaol ♣, which was demolished in 1902, shortly after this photograph was taken, and replaced by the Central Criminal Court.

OPEN SPACES

In 1872 Blanchard Jerrold wrote, in his *London, A Pilgrimage,* 'Surely, the most obstinate and prejudiced traducer of London must admit that the Cockney is well provided with greenery. The picturesqueness of the St James's and Regent's Parks, and of Kensington Gardens, is not to be matched by any capital with which I am familiar, or of which I have heard. In these open places there are sylvan views, that carry the mind and heart hundreds of miles from the noise and dirt of Cheapside.'

Jerrold was in fact describing the greenery in a very small patch of fashionable London. There had been much concern at the speed with which London's fields and green spaces were being covered with building, and the fact that many of the poorest families were denied even the smallest space for their children to play. Greens or commons disappeared in Chelsea, Lambeth, Stockwell and many other places, which led to urgent action with the creation of parks (many were partial survivals of old open spaces, enclosed) which were open to all. These included Alexandra Park, Clissold Park, Victoria Park, Battersea Park and Waterlow Park. Heaths, commons and woods were also acquired and saved for posterity as at Epping, Hampstead, Putney, Hornsey and Clapham. On a smaller scale, some of the old city burial grounds were converted to gardens. These were badly needed for the inhabitants of the most overcrowded and slum-ridden parts of London. There was one in Drury Lane, and another in St Giles near the notorious Seven Dials, both 'planted and opened as any outdoor sitting-room'.

Above left: *HYDE PARK. A view of The Drive, Rotten Row and The Promenade on the southern side of Hyde Park where fashionable London took the air. The writer Blanchard Jerrold described the riders as 'the gently born and gently nurtured, driving the heat and faintness of ball-room out, by spirited canters through a grove of such green leaves as only our well-abused English climate can produce.' The Drive was used by the carriages, the Row by equestrians and the Promenade by pedestrians, who for the price of a penny might stop and sit on a chair.*

Above right: *HYDE PARK CORNER. A view looking over to Park Lane, from the grandest entrance to the Park just by Apsley House. Jerrold continued: 'Hyde Park at the height of the season; Hyde Park on an afternoon when the Four-in-Hand Club is out in full force, is the best picture that we can present to a stranger, of the pride and wealth, the blood and bearing, the comeliness, beauty, and metal of Old England.'*

Right: *THE ROUND POND AT KENSINGTON GARDENS, where Victorian children sailed their model boats under the watchful eyes of their nursemaids. Kensington Gardens were first laid out by William III while he lived in Kensington Palace. They were much enjoyed by Queen Caroline, wife of George II, so she appropriated an extra three hundred acres or so from Hyde Park and engaged the most fashionable landscape gardener of the day, Charles Bridgeman, to create a new layout for them. It was at this point that many of the avenues were planted and the Serpentine was created.*

*THE ROYAL BOTANIC GARDENS, KEW.
The leaves of the gigantic Victoria
Regina waterlily float in the huge
tank in the Tropical House of the
Royal Botanic Gardens. Experiments
proved that the leaves were able to
bear the weight of a man. Intrepid
Victorian plant hunters sent their
specimens to Kew and these were
nurtured by the botanists in the
glasshouses, meticulously maintained
at the correct temperatures.*

*THE ZOOLOGICAL GARDENS IN REGENT'S
PARK were visited by over 600,000
people in 1894, by which time they
had become known simply as the
'Zoo'. Animals such as Jumbo the
Indian elephant, who arrived with
his mate Alice in 1867, were much
photographed and extremely
popular, and new arrivals were
closely scrutinised. Sunday
afternoon was the busiest time,
when gentlemen would escort ladies
while carrying a chair for them in
case they desired to sit down. 'It is
the very place for quiet easy talk in
the open air – with animals to point
the conversation. The sentimental
linger by the gazelles: the hoyden
makes merry with the parrots: the
humourists gather in the monkey
house: the muscular-minded
Amazon watches old Leo rasping the
shin-bone with his rough tongue.'*

LINCOLN'S INN FIELDS were saved from being built over through the endeavours of the members of Lincoln's Inn, who objected to development plans which were proposed during the reign of Charles I. The land had originally been playing fields for the students of Lincoln's Inn, so it had long served as place of recreation (although it had also been the site of executions as late as 1683). By the end of the nineteenth century it was a rare open space in the middle of the capital which provided fresh air and space for those living in the 'crowded courts of Drury Lane and its vicinity'.

Left: *EMBANKMENT GARDENS were caused by one of the most dramatic improvements to Victorian London. This was the construction during the 1860s and 1870s of the three miles of stone embankment along the previously muddy and marshy banks of the Thames. The reclaimed land below the Strand was turned into gardens, and named the Victoria Embankment Gardens. Among the attractions were a bandstand and Cleopatra's Needle. The caption to the 1896 publication of this photograph reads: 'On a fine summer's day they are crowded with idlers and loungers, some of whom are there for pleasure, and many because they have nothing better to do.'*

Inset, top left: *FOUNTAIN COURT, THE TEMPLE - 'Between busy Fleet Street and the stately Embankment are found a venerable church, magnificent Gothic halls, piles of stately buildings, dull old quadrangles, spacious lawns, clumps of old trees, blooming gardens, and a sweet, shady nook, where a little fountain plays in the midst of rockeries and flowers . . . which resounds on a summer's evening with the merry laughter of hundreds of little children who are allowed to play there by the Benchers, or principal authorities of the Temple.'*

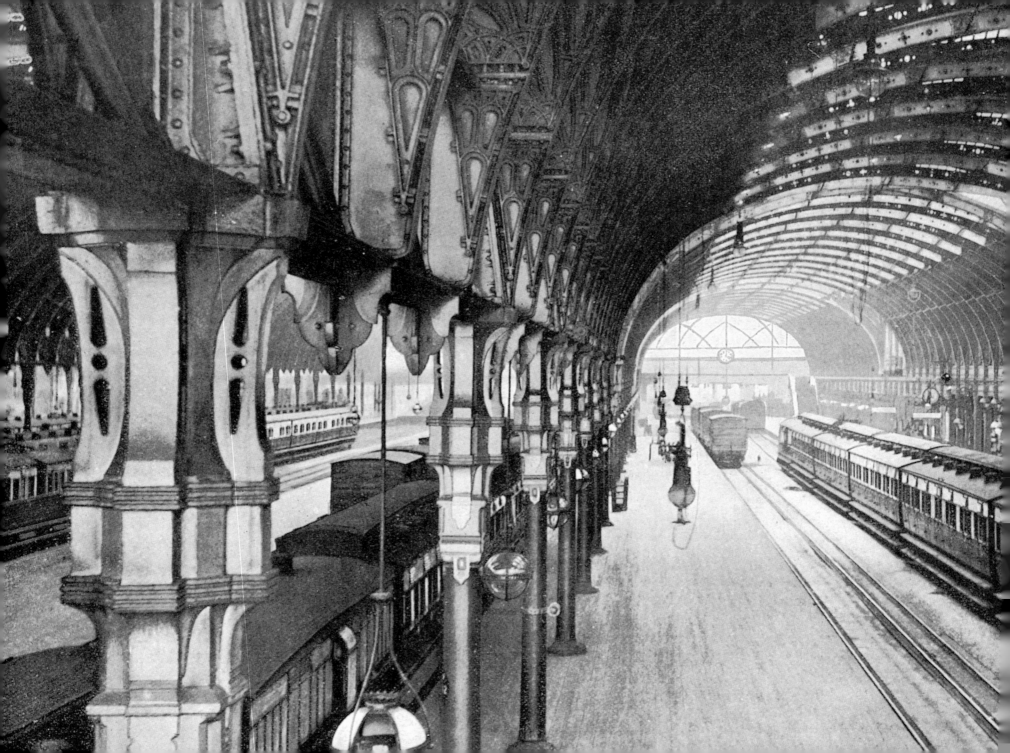

THE RAILWAYS

By the end of the nineteenth century the railways reigned supreme, changing dramatically the way in which people travelled, in terms not only of speed, but also of comfort. G.A. Sala wrote a book entitled *London up to Date* in 1894; he first described the scene in front of the big London stations: 'There is a big yard in front of the premises; and this yard, for full sixteen hours out of the twenty-four, is thronged with heavily-laden omnibuses, hansoms, and four-wheelers, private carriages, carts, and vans, all coming from and going, seemingly, in opposite directions, and productive of a distressing amount of noise, confusion, and unreportable language.'

However, he could see no end to this extraordinary new age: 'wheresoever we travel, we find more extensive, more elaborate arrangements made for enabling passengers to refect themselves comfortably at their leisure, luxuriously, and without exorbitant charge.' He particularly admired the Pullman breakfast train by which he travelled from Brighton to London, leaving at 8.45 and arriving at Victoria at 10.05. On this he was offered buttered toast, boiled egg, fried sole, broiled ham, kidneys, bloaters or haddock, 'succulent, well served and inexpensive.'

PADDINGTON STATION was built shortly after the Great Exhibition, a fitting terminus for Isambard Kingdom Brunel's Great Western Railway. His design for the station, with its great arched construction, was partly inspired by the Crystal Palace. The trains introduced by the GWR in 1892 were much admired: '. . . the corridor train, which combines the distinctive merits of the British and American patterns. In this kind of train there are smoking saloons and toilet-rooms, and the carriages are warmed by waste steam from the engine.'

EUSTON STATION was opened in 1837. Successive improvements and additions meant that by 1849 it was considered to be a very impressive spectacle, and crowds of sightseers travelled by omnibus from all over London to inspect it. It was the terminus of the London and North-Western Railway, with profitable lines such as the west coast route to Scotland. By the 1890s the company had its own steamers carrying the mail between Holyhead and Dublin and the Scotch Express mail train 'which is considered the most wonderful train in the world.'

KING'S CROSS, the London terminus of the Great Northern Railway, which was opened in 1852. Due to the lack of ornamentation on its façade it was considered architecturally very dull. However, its storage capacity was impressive: a granary capable of holding 60,000 sacks of corn, water-tanks capable of holding 150,000 gallons and coal stores that would hold over 15,200 tons.

VICTORIA STATION, a view of the station yard at the terminus of the London, Brighton and South Coast Railway. This was also the arrival point for travellers from Continental Europe, who an observer noted could not fail to be impressed with 'a sense of the bewildering energy of our mighty city' by the sight of the omnibuses from all quarters of the Metropolis and enormous cab traffic in the station yard.

LIVERPOOL STREET, at the entrance to the railway station, the terminus for the Great Eastern, North London, and London and North-Western Railways. This station was widely used by people commuting into the City, and as many as 110,000 people were using it daily by the 1890s.

THE MIDLAND GRAND HOTEL at
ST. PANCRAS, which was completed in
1876. Almost the entire slum
neighbourhood known as Agar Town
was demolished to make way for
St Pancras, which was considered an
architectural triumph: 'It must be
owned that, towering as it does to
into mid-air, it is the most beautiful
structure, and stands without a rival
for palatial beauty, comfort and
convenience . . . There are bedrooms
for upwards of 500 guests; and the
Hotel, with its fittings and furniture,
cannot have cost less than half a
million sterling.'

THE CHARING CROSS HOTEL was built
at the same time as the railway
station, in 1864. It had 210
bedrooms, and was very highly
considered, in particular for its
magnificent dining room. The
architect, E. M. Barry, also supplied
a replica of the medieval Eleanor
Cross, which can be seen in the
forecourt. The original was erected
by King Edward I to mark the last
resting place of the funeral cortege
on its way to Westminster Abbey in
1290.

THE GROSVENOR HOTEL, from which it was possible to descend directly to the platforms of Victoria Station. It was pointed out that, being in the heart of Belgravia, this hotel, built in 1861, was superior to other railway hotels. Also, if one were travelling to it in winter from Hyde Park Corner on the top of an omnibus, it might sometimes be possible to see the Royal Family skating on the frozen ponds of Buckingham Palace gardens.

Right: CANNON STREET STATION AND HOTEL belonged to the South-Eastern Railway company, for whom it was their City terminus. This position, north of the Thames, and centrally placed in the City, was designed especially for the growing numbers of commuters. There was also a convenient connection by subway with the Metropolitan District Railway, which had just extended the line to Wimbledon in 1889.

RESIDENTIAL LONDON

PRINCE'S GATE, KENSINGTON, was built in the middle of the nineteenth century as part of the development surrounding the Great Exhibition's Crystal Palace in Hyde Park. Prince Albert conceived this part of town as an area of excellence, with four museums, a concert hall and colleges of science, art and music. These substantial red brick houses appealed to a number of newly wealthy families who wished to live in London, and at a fashionable address. Some moved away from living in the City, which was at that time considered socially unacceptable. A contemporary description states: 'It is vain to look for any ancient buildings in this part of London; there is nothing to be seen but apparently interminable vistas of five-storied palaces, past which roll elegant carriages conveying their wealthy occupants on shopping expeditions, to theatres, and to social functions generally.'

The considerable growth in the population of London during the second half of the nineteenth century is a well-known fact, and the reasons various and complex. Among the most obvious are the move of many agricultural workers from the country into the town to search for work as the 1860s depression in agriculture bit deep; the growth of a middle class for the increased number of office, clerking and bureaucratic jobs; and an increase in the number of ambitious newly rich Victorians who could afford to sample the pleasures of Society and life in the capital. The development of the underground and overground railways meant that areas which had hitherto been villages on the edge of London became satellite suburbs and developers quickly filled in any green space between town and village with the ubiquitous Victorian terrace. This came in a variety of sizes ranging from the six-storey grandeur of Belgravia and Kensington to the two-bedroom artisans' cottages put up near the railway in Camden. However, since the wealthy households could not function without a surrounding infrastructure of shops, servants and services, the streets of London were surprisingly mixed. A social investigator named Charles Booth published a map of London at the end of the century in which he coloured all the streets according to the inhabitants: these ranged from 'semi-criminal' (black) and very poor (dark blue) through to comfortable (brown), well-to-do (red) and wealthy (gold). What is clear is that one group never lived more than a few streets away from another.

GUINNESS LODGING-HOUSES ♣ , LEVER STREET, Finsbury, were built in the early 1890s for the urban poor in a determined effort by the philanthropic Sir Edward Guinness to improve their living conditions. Even at the end of the century there were still Londoners living in slum conditions in the old courts and alleys, 'where squalid misery and poverty struggle with filth and wretchedness, where vice reigns unchecked, and in the atmosphere of which the worst diseases are generated and diffused, as Sir Walter Besant wrote in 1909. This building housed about 1,400 people, providing single rooms for two shillings per week plus the use of a club-room with newspapers and games, hot and cold water baths, boiling water for teapots at mealtimes and hot water for washing at all hours of the day. This was a considerable improvement on the old slum areas where the water was only turned on for an hour or two each day.

LONDON COUNTY COUNCIL LODGING-HOUSES, *Parker Street, Covent Garden. These were erected with in five years of the establishment of the L.C.C. to house 324 men who were charged sixpence a night in 1896 for a cubicle to sleep in. In addition there was a kitchen, where the men could prepare food for themselves, a reading-room, work room, lavatories and bath rooms, a washhouse for clothes and a day-room 'where they can smoke, read, play chess or draughts, and are entertained by weekly concerts during the winter months'.*

Right: 5 HAMILTON PLACE, a view from the tennis court of Mr Leopold de Rothschild's town house just off Picadilly, which he had built about fifteen years before this photograph was taken. His neighbours included Lord Eldon and the Duchess of Sutherland; next door was the Bachelors' Club where Prince Henry of Battenberg had lived before he married Princess Beatrice, Queen Victoria's youngest daughter.

Far right: SPENCER HOUSE, a view from Green Park. One of the finest of the London town houses, built for John, 1st Earl Spencer in 1766 and worked on by some of the finest architects and furniture makers of the day. By the end of the nineteenth century it was 'at present rented by Mr Barney Barnato, the South African millionaire, pending completion of his own house in Park Lane.'

Left: *DORCHESTER HOUSE* ♣, *PARK LANE*. Below left: *DUDLEY HOUSE, PARK LANE*. *Park Lane was one of the best addresses in London. The 'modern mansion' Dorchester House was built on the site of the Marquess of Hertford's old town house for a millionaire named R.S.Holford, who filled it with paintings by Van Dyck, Velasquez, Murillo and Titian. It was rented to the Shahzada of Afghanistan, who visited London in 1895, for the astonishing sum of £1,000 per week. Dudley House was built for Lord Dudley in the 1820s at the time when the family income from its coal-mining interests alone was £30,000 a year. By the end of the century the house belonged to the 'well-known South African millionaire, Mr J. B. Robinson, the friend of President Kruger.'*

Below: *MONTAGU HOUSE* ♣, *a view from Whitehall. The Duke of Buccleuch built this in 1863 on the site of an 'insignificant' house that he had inherited from the Montagu family and immediately demolished. Its magnificent appearance was greatly admired: 'So noble is the appearance of this mansion that even the great Government buildings close by cannot eclipse it.'*

Left: CHESTERFIELD HOUSE ♣, a Palladian mansion built for the Earl of Chesterfield in 1749. He incorporated, at vast expense, a grand staircase and the marble columns round the courtyard, from Canons Park in Edgware, a house that had been recently demolished by the bankrupt Duke of Chandos. Chesterfield House was under threat of demolition in the 1860s but was bought by a wealthy city merchant named Magniac. It was finally demolished in 1937.

Below: HOLLAND HOUSE, a Jacobean mansion built in the village of Kensington in 1607 for Sir Walter Cope, who passed it on to his son-in-law the Earl of Holland. The Hollands were a prominent Whig family and the house became the centre of political intrigue during the seventeenth and eighteenth centuries. Ten years before this photograph was taken the house was inherited by Lord Ilchester, who with his wife gave famous garden parties, balls and fêtes. Most of the house was destroyed by a bomb during the Second World War.

MONUMENTS

When the new garden on the Embankment of the Thames was completed, it was much admired, but one commentator significantly suggested that there were not enough statues ornamenting it. The nineteenth century was the great age of the Monument and the Memorial. Clearly earlier ones existed, such as that built after the Fire of London, but in the main they were Victorian additions. The Victorians were not slow either to give historical figures their due – hence Richard Coeur de Lion outside the Palace of Westminster and Shakespeare in Leicester Square – or to celebrate more recent heroes and heroines, such as Wellington outside the Royal Exchange, Sir Robert Peel ✣ in Cheapside, and Florence Nightingale in Waterloo Place. Probably the most commemorated figure of all was Prince Albert, whose early death sent the Queen into mourning for at least fifteen years. The most spectacular memorial is the Albert Memorial at the site of the Great Exhibition; it was designed by Sir Gilbert Scott and took a good twenty years to complete at a cost of over £130,000. A rather more modest statue was erected at Holborn Circus.

Left: THE MONUMENT *was built at the behest of Charles II to commemorate the Great Fire of London in 1666. Sir Christopher Wren designed it and within eleven years it was erected; at 202 feet it dominated the skyline of London for the next two and a half centuries. In 1896 it required a payment of threepence to climb the interior spiral staircase of 345 black marble steps to see the city from the viewing platform.*

LORD BEACONSFIELD'S STATUE, Parliament Square; Queen Victoria created her favourite Prime Minister, Benjamin Disraeli, Earl of Beaconsfield in 1876, five years before his death. This photograph shows how his statue looked on Primrose Day, when it was decorated with a mass of his favourite flowers. 'Peace with Honour' refers to Disraeli's diplomatic triumph at the Congress of Berlin in 1878, when he agreed a peace treaty between Russia and Turkey and obtained control of Cyprus for Great Britain.

Right: THE DUKE OF YORK'S COLUMN, viewed from the Mall. This memorial to the Duke of York was erected in the 1830s. Brother to George IV and King William IV, and uncle to Queen Victoria, he was a popular Commander-in-Chief of the Army until he was forced to resign after a scandal revealed that his mistress, Mrs Clark, had accepted bribes to secure commissions. The column is about 20 feet shorter than Nelson's, but jokes current at the time of its building suggested that it was high enough to keep the Duke safe from his famously numerous creditors. By the time this photograph was taken the public had been stopped from climbing on to the platform at the top by means of the internal spiral staircase.

Far right: THE ALBERT MEMORIAL was completed in 1876, fourteen years after the notion of a national memorial to the Prince had been agreed upon. The Queen picked the design by George Gilbert Scott from a selection submitted by the foremost architects of the day. The gilded statue of the Prince sits under its Gothic canopy profusely decorated with mosaic, enamel, polished stone and elaborate metalwork. The edifice is flanked with sculpture 'illustrating those works, arts and sciences which he fostered, and the great under-takings which he originated'. The whole enclosure is marked with monumental marble groups personifying Europe, Asia, America and Africa.

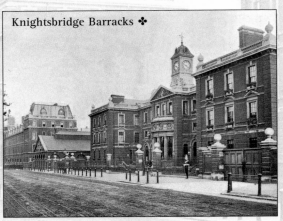

Knightsbridge Barracks ✤

BIBLIOGRAPHY

Walter Besant *London in the Nineteenth Century* (London, 1909)

Walter Besant *London North of the Thames* (London, 1911)

Gustav Dore and Blanchard Jerrold *London, A Pilgrimage* (London, 1872)

Juliet Gardiner *Queen Victoria* (London 1997)

Peter Jackson *Walks in Old London* (London, 1993)

(Eds.) Nikolaus Pevsner and Bridget Cherry *The Buildings of England, London* (London, revised editions 1973, 1991)

George Augustus Sala *London up to Date* (London, 1894)

Christopher Simon Sykes *Private Palaces, Life in the Great London Houses* (London, 1985)

Gavin Weightman *Bright Lights, Big City, London Entertained 1830-1950* (London, 1992)

Gavin Weightman *London River* (London, 1990)

Gavin Weightman and Steve Humphries *The Making of Modern London 1815-1914* (London 1983)

(Eds.) Ben Weinreb and Christopher Hibbert *The London Encyclopaedia* (London, 1983)

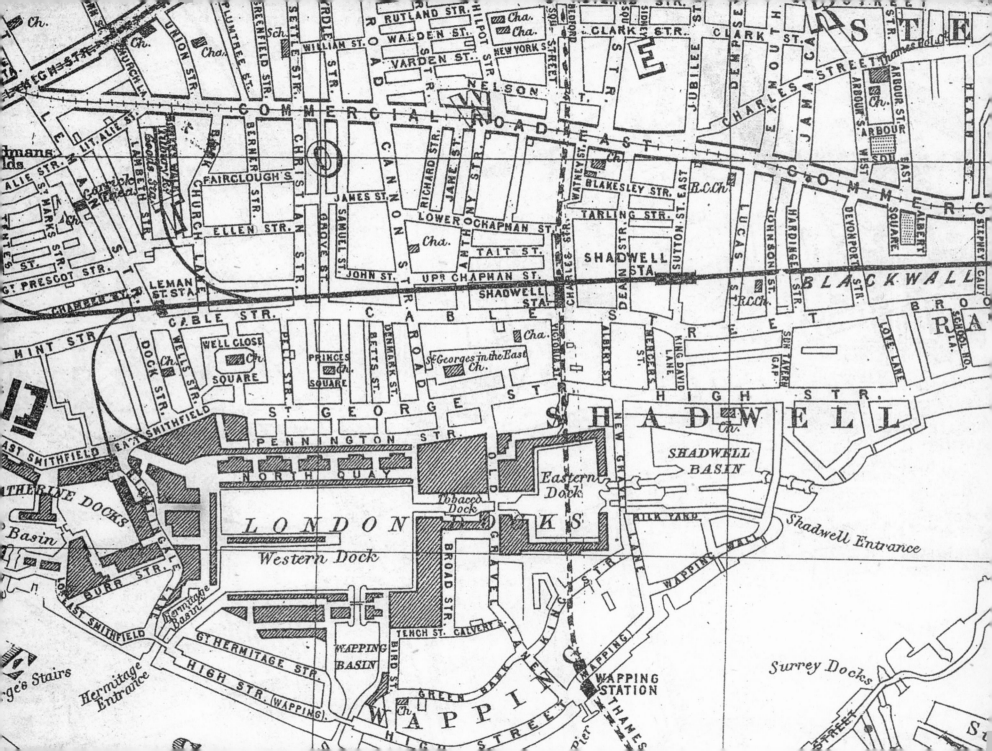